T0282993

INFINITY POOL

PHOENIX POETS

Edited by Srikanth Reddy

Rosa Alcalá, Douglas Kearney &

Katie Peterson, consulting editors

Infinity Pool

JONATHAN THIRKIELD

THE UNIVERSITY OF CHICAGO PRESS
CHICAGO & LONDON

The University of Chicago Press, Chicago 60637
The University of Chicago Press, Ltd., London
©2024 by The University of Chicago
All rights reserved. No part of this book may be used or reproduced in any manner whatsoever
without written permission, except in the case of brief quotations in critical articles and reviews.
For more information, contact the University of Chicago Press, 1427 E. 60th St., Chicago, IL 60637.
Published 2024
Printed in the United States of America

33 32 31 30 29 28 27 26 25 24   1 2 3 4 5

ISBN-13: 978-0-226-83477-1 (paper)
ISBN-13: 978-0-226-83478-8 (e-book)
DOI: https://doi.org/10.7208/chicago/9780226834788.001.0001

Library of Congress Cataloging-in-Publication Data

Names: Thirkield, Jonathan, 1973– author.
Title: Infinity pool / Jonathan Thirkield.
Other titles: Phoenix poets.
Description: Chicago ; London : The University of Chicago Press, 2024. | Series: Phoenix poets
Identifiers: LCCN 2023050516 | ISBN 9780226834771 (paperback) | ISBN 9780226834788 (ebook)
Subjects: LCGFT: Poetry.
Classification: LCC PS3620.H57 I54 2024 | DDC 811/.6—dc23/eng/20231106
LC record available at https://lccn.loc.gov/2023050516

♾ This paper meets the requirements of ANSI/NISO Z39.48-1992 (Permanence of Paper).

for E, C & I

Phantomatics stands for creating bidirectional links between the "artificial reality" and its recipient. In other words, phantomatics is a feedback art. . . . Phantomatics stands for creating situations in which there are no "exits" from the worlds of created fiction into the real world.

STANISŁAW LEM, Summa Technologiae, 1964

CONTENTS

...

Deep Mind 5
Perceptron 7
Phantomatics 9
Deep Dream 10
Thinking Machine 12
To a Kid Launched One Year after the iPhone 14

...

Voyager 19
The Atlas of Virtual 20
Coma 25
Ecosphere 26
Icarus 27
Infinity Pool 30

...

Lyme Chronicles 35

...

Virtual Terminal 47
Antwerp 48
Persephone 53
Albedo 55
<graywithmoonlight> 56
Moon Pool 58
Antwerp 61

. . .

Super Fragile Catalyst 69

Acknowledgments 81
Notes 83

INFINITY POOL

Deep Mind

mimic soul mimic shoals
school of flesh

pool of mirrors
beveled melodic strain

at the edge nodes
bent and rendered

crushed luster blissed
in starry clusters

dream steeped leap
from cliffs caught

in neural nets'
convolution layers

to the pooling level
further filtered smoothing

down the feature maps
are you learning

are you here
do your ears work

do your eyes light up
how does sound hum

from the windpipe
where do you hide

the memory stains
cursive script

of lips distilled
to archways sound shapes

spheres of effluence
streaming wet air

humid heart humid liver
patterns pass play

through the ossicles
verse chorus verse pulse

beet berry legume
bloom breath brine

rime forms
on rinds

Perceptron

node and thread
the eye the mouth

the oval range and tilt
of recognition coded

deep into the frame
a mind is primed

to seek a mirror face
draw its safe attachment

test the thresholds
by gradient descent

what is the rain
spelling welling

drumbeat drowns out
rounds down

the body to skin
surface boundaries

abstracts the latticework
cloud systems

skull stems
tree cortex

axis vertex
fusiform gyrus

branch into creases
rivulets gutter gather

topographic patter
leak along the cheek

a leaf touched
thought a sea

Phantomatics

bright green womb
automated heartbeat

sentimental mint jellies
dayglo tulip syrup

uranium fingerpainting
ultraviolet lighterfluid

tone by tone
new and viral

jar of rubles
five and dim

spool of lead
sleet of cotton

silk ink sky
disinformation

Deep Dream

dissolve the camera's eye
to ghost the riband wave

two pencil mark eyelets
at the wing's fringe

may make a face a place
an initial position

in a stochastic plot
a pause a grain

random walk mid May lost
in decision trees

random forest black wash
tiled kite and strand

and feather ever listing
glistening twist

and whirl the will
erased in tide glazed

sand paths tempered
to cut glass panes

mottled in grit silt
slits through which

ghost nodes crash
catch clusters of yes

of what gaze what hand
what changed stage or state

of self pours through
solves true trills

to unlit weather dazed
operations guesses

gusts gates and gullies
weights ever measured

recalibrated hardened
arteries thick pith flecked

architecture vector texture
how real to feel

the ashen sky signs drift
on its spectral surface

Thinking Machine

overlord motherboard
pinball wizard vector swarm

self assembling
coherence engine

lithe electric watercourse
dark arcade meat maze

color shifting anole
mood ring lizard

rabbit warren bee cathedral
termite palace

time bomb skull bulb
planted fist deep

in wet earth
fed letters fetters

wish deep in gest
kiss me at the neck

a fleck of red
lights up

the gray meter
lyric slip aglitter

slide a slice
of lemon round

a highball's lip
salt crowned

shadow gowned
wrist wrapped

in crystal thistle tines
glance up the spine

spike lush currents
tessellate emergent

landscape portrait fortress
porous verse chorus thirst

I only sing well
to the people I love

To a Kid Launched One Year after the iPhone

Summery over the last few years, sparrows casting
Quarter and eighth notes on the mulberry leaves,
Someone in an empire waist Sunday cotton
Strawberry pastel, shoeless, tulips, slate dust
On the pads of her feet, oatmeal cooling, caking,
Honey colored kitchen, buttons falling
From my sleeves, everything is writing

Feathers through the pillow linings, puffed up lungs,
Voyager passing through our stellar cloud, robot
Sleepwalkers/rock combers, sea-blue sky,
Sky-blue sea, tide up, handheld technologies
Coming soon to change us, rain counts up
From one to twenty million pixels filling in
The film we're in, maybe I'm rewriting the whole

Thing right as I watch it, time won't release
The sequel till it's ready, centripetal marketing
Keeps the blips from passing through the firewall
Of the future, birds in the storm drain wearing
Our interiors out, hot in pettiness, sweeping image
After image across the table, trees segmented
Into emulsions of light and bark. Who lies at the center

Of your body, makes the tremor of unknowing
In the purple wing and rib cage? I didn't realize
How long I'd flowed through the flea market,
I wasn't feeling myself. "Their skin
Is green and lit up from within," a boy
Says, holding my hand, thinking he belongs
To me, I resemble others, we wander

Past carpet hangings, the watches
And necklaces plumbing the blue gravy
Table folds, glass cases display evidence
Of our preexistence, I may have
Been a bulb on a string of lights before
I became people. I keep telling the boy not
To worry, we will find him a present.

"Cats are like ninjas," he says.
"Little ninjas with four feet."
A row of ancient toy joints and levers
Half-working. Maybe I'll keep him. Milk
Crates with slipcovered stills, a photograph
Of an actor sells in a heartbeat. I look
At the boy (cells and a heartbeat) when did I start
Telling time by the size of his body?

Soon, we'll have an app to sync the heartbeats of all three
Billion unique users. Soon, image captures will construct
Mosaics of the three billion fields of vision
Corresponding to each heartbeat. Soon, each present
Will feel identical to the next. You stand in
The kitchen in an empire waist honey colored
Lace, among books of others, sometimes binding

Yourself to them, sometimes like you are looking
At me through a pill suppressing the current
Of sensation of unlikeliness, the whole room
Having been modified by adjectives, a straw
Pressed through an orange, small body,
Sparrow sized, underneath bolts
Of textiles, the transition from being

Lost to building a set of prescribed rules
For forgetting, invisible railroads
Pushing you toward the haptic surface
Sensors, unable to shake off your
Digital fingerprints despite the soft
Palm taking up half your hand, as you think
You guide its body through its particular line of sight.

. . .

Voyager

Future men with neon bones glowing through their taupe pigmentation,

Graphite suits, grapefruit sized eyes, graphene carbon circuits flowing code

Through their pores, shadows with falsetto voices, silhouette marionette

Cardboard placards for souls like they're bearing a kiosk, a pixel of water

Sparkling for a second inside the pinhole cell wall of their pupils,

New moons somewhere where light disappears, boys, blue ink pouring

Through their veins, shout into wells, some with echoes, some without,

The waves of their voices crash on us here, on this shore of, at the edge

Of the words you hear, and back into old brick men, arms of iron ore,

Frozen ancient bearded ones, all white and crystalline, yellow fossilized

Irises, forked-lightning veins radiating from the chest, fingerprints

Written into the clouds, a sky like cotton pulled apart in ink covered hands.

The Atlas of Virtual

Constantly recorded, listening through loops
Of string of blue with fraying fibers webbing
The walls of the kitchen, climbing like ivy
Into the ears of our loved ones, channels
Playing whales and spinning light-up
Jellyfish, lipstick headed tubers by the ocean's
Vents, music making modulated intimations

Of the lives of minor species, brown and golden red
Across the white paged sky, a tablet
Of numbers spiraling out from one like trapdoors
Beneath a stage where a table stands with settings in Dutch blue
Of Japanese castles, cypresses, blue brick walls
Dividing the pastures, cows, sheep, a stray deer
Nibbling at an apple, and a huntsman in sandals

Drawing his bow, the feet of children showing
Beneath a fence by the stable playing
Harpsichords, samisens and sitars on the service
Platter, tiny sketches of robotic spy insects
Twitching in the marsh, and I grew hungry, I ripped
The greenest lowest branch and loosest chips,
The skin of moss at its foot, forgetting that trees

Are others, forgetting people are always close
And listening, the mountains drilled through for
Fiberoptic trains, hidden suns speeding a desire for
Water, speeding the sleepless heart with particulate
Matter, the regions of dust in the visual apnea where
Mother and starlet and cow blend within the segmented
Caterpillar rushes, all seeping into the deepest troughs

Of the river systems of Mars, beneath the Olympus
Mons, the pyramidal tracts, a system of green men
With leaflike pinnate ears harvesting root crops
In the sub-rosa villages. During my abduction, the one
I'd prayed for all those years under the painted girl
Whispering, you are special, you really are,
Not an apparition in my night window, the six lights

From the hydroelectric plant making a crown
Above her many eyes. I toured the catacombs
Under the sandy planetary face, nothing was
Illusion, they called my guide Virtual, their towers
Modeled on a neurotransit system, trains
Passed from axon to dendrite, the supple liquid
Walls teeming with krill-like ground creatures,

They said, snack as you please. The taste bordered
On pork rinds and blueberries, the redder ones were
Sweeter, almost cotton candy, for a minute every
Word rhymed with every other one, the poison ones
Are irresistible and equally unstable, they said,
Approaching the planet's nuclear heart or amygdala,
Its marzipan scent covering field upon field of dark

Tentacular flowers or ideas, I couldn't tell, the smell
So enveloped my senses like a boat crashing through
The snowy skullcap of a Western child, I thought
Briefly the Martians wore Japanese teddy bear
Suits, even heard the zippers close up their spines and felt
Myself being enclosed in one as well, it was difficult
To see through the pinhole eye, my head became

A camera obscura, I watched the film of a mariner
Eating bodies he carved with an LCD glass machete
That played video collages culled by a spider
Algorithm: a roulette of babies, cats, mirror
Soliloquies, violinists in short dresses, cooking
Instructions, nuptials, snake v. mongoose, poverty
Trials, cucumbers on the eyes, centers getting

Posterized, and a very long song about May. I may
Have been in the bear head for seconds or years being fed
By the mariner. The many men, so beautiful,
I feared, but I ate and ate, because they reassured
Me it was a dream, all of it, the scented watermelon
On the shoulders of the women, the scent of quinine
On their feathers, the myriad reductions—wine, cherry,

Anise—bubbling up from the skin, the fading purgatory
Impulse as my hunger and joy took hold. I felt perfect
Complicity with the mariner, he was the reason
I thought, the reason words gave way to pictures again,
He was the manager of the bodies. I came to
An oasis, Virtual let me surf the liquid plasma,
The buttons on her face went purple-pink, the doctor lost

His horse in the snow, and a trainer applied oleoresin
To his client's thighs. The answer to every office pool,
The runoff from every dye job, the diminishing, ever
Diminishing trees and catalysts and rare earth
Materials seemed to extend their private wilds
Into an infinite number of vanishing points. It
Was or it wasn't. I was told a girl in the farmlands

Of China had lied to her friends about owning
A horse, said her brother put him down just yesterday
And showed them the patch of grass: blood, hoofprint
And all. I was told to visit her with a lead-glazed heart filled
With aphids. I was told to write things down with a Sharpie
Every morning on the surface of the water,
And when I did, the words became affixed to my

Forehead. For days I wrote *anabasis*, thinking it
Meant something else. Virtual was pleased. Thirty
Days or hours or lives of purple sky passed over
Me, lambs and squires rested in the fields like
White chocolate daubs on a macaroon, my skin
Broke out in gray eruptions, I was told this was
A common reaction to snow. The stars finally cut

Through the purple silk, I was told this too
happened to visitors, visitors who forced
Their memory of Earth's weather and atmospheric
Anomalies on the entoptically dense ferry terminals
Of the Martian life terrines. I was told stories
Of microcuisines, services in petri dishes, blue
Liquid racing down from droppers to make things

More palatable. I was told of the 47 facial expressions
And the withdrawal of love after the first 108
Days of life, the phloem and xylem that mediate
The memory hinges. Virtual was curious about all
Those home movies, film ones, from the seventies
With the bleached light, memory light, those silences
And vacancies, roadside hotels of killing music,

Polypropylene quilts, black and white kids
In matching T-shirts, the owl brown of the trees
Corroding the film stock, the centripetal desire
Of watching those endless false battles in Japanese
On Saturdays, and the difference between moths
And paper as both emerge from tree life, and pattern
Themselves on language, and die when wet.

Coma

as the volume turned down just below one seems silent
and the readout on the stereo still rises and falls like model cities
the body's brain waves may play some natural background noise

as if the cosmos were singing a billion tiny things to us
which the needle on the record's edge records
but we don't have the language to restore:

the moon revolves around the sun, the living
around the nearly gone, her mind around itself
because there's nowhere else to go, no walking through those waves

to some unconscious shore, the illusion that you are
your body fades, that when they turn off the machines, the stems
won't continue thirsting for music thinking by water

Ecosphere

Spider, cider, and delight
A shell goes spinning from the spine.
Quiet empyrean, five petaled zones
Fanning out from the solar fold.
A brimstone alights
On a primrose, yellow fleck
On yellow flame.
The snail slips up the apple skin,
Crowded planet of souls.

Nations inscribe plantations and mines
Into X-ray maps
Of our interiors: bulbs, blurs, and masses
Suspended in sugar coded spheres of water.
Vapor rising from a spring.
Arbitrary coloring.
A body under snowfall gathers text
And time in some imaginary order.

Icarus

gunite false sea gray arena double diluted whistle cuneiform wave applets

run object

eddy

screen pass long bomb

azure shallows

arcade court kids elide

read write splash input output cache cash cast reflections skim ripple

city set arrays out impact early plated crofts

pockets of wool

bleats

a hint of desert before tan wisteria boxwood moonlight melanin in stadia written

over zero

moss whittled the digital rainfall willy-nilly

alabaman sweet gum flowering

dint of cataplectic burying

exchange

drainage

diminish

wilt the family shape and oval tarps in liquid dollar netting an inertial puck floats

stick to stick across the planes of coolants crystal hooded data stock gray

wire the parchment field silver

if it's early if the neuroblast anew maps to

fiery callow video section escarpments barricade permeance pinging the plasma cell

frame into the sealants glow distortion returning as a culture shifts in swift

blots

lumens trans eye speed freezing in all warring passages slip entries to the version's

surface flow

vertically loved

yesterly

fastened imprinted

loved a long lung

before the floriated bedrooms ran in the first wild clearings of dynamite quilted

travel speeding inflorescences

as to perceive the magic of the body like a wall of visual dirt shares

the office always awaiting a view revinyled yellow padded prairie navel bliss
you
moving a kite in the brush
tending its quaint thinned vision along the pathways
minutemen
silvery trillium
a lead paste stain
alum acrobat neatly derendering the suburban halos
looped samples over the crash chart's flat invention of a cross
sputter and wind
downpour
mast cells pass the roll fantasy column
i dream you to become you
spread of subway silos
living body on a dry lake
ring after knockout
to a suede glyphed lawn course
quill instrumental cleft
babel
event
babel
event
boy gull
gamble fallow
father son signage surviving the surf
waiting
wading
wilting dew rises off the tentpole trailers
summer pictures
release dates
way off higher than your teeth flood
common gold capped carpenter lock stack
rip of code patches
skeletal wakes in retrieval

pathogen bricks flick apocalypse gifs
recursive systems sifted feudal immune delusions telemetry consoles
splice virus on virus in exponential quotients flash bubble on the retinal foil
delivery din membrane meme branch organ grain dna polymerase pyrosequencing
mortal combat silica ocean glow and fret on the seventh string's wings without us
i love you
forsaking naming
i love you
as if you were nothing
a whale walking candle tallow in warm salt seasons of small cap melt i feel our time
closing off the hope motorboats would disappear a hope for traditional predators
that our bodies and manias would be useful to the seafloor
fresher
mosaic tiles
planted by a lawyer
more natural than the mind could claim ownership dawn
babel
event
babel
refresh

. . .

Infinity Pool

Strings of discontinued monarch utterances in the memory aisle
by the dulcet Wal-Mart atrium adjacent to a stunningly moving

stretch of booths at the art liquidator's fair in the Columbus Meridian:
opulent earrings, desolate lulls in the brain willows, carrion upon

the shoulders, lace over the façade, a head swapped with a circuit
on an androgynous set of twins beautiful enough to be caged and wheeled

through the palaces of your bedrooms to the view of an infinity pool;
a crimson river of stop-motion rubies, lunular scythe-ends over

the fermata's pupil, shapeless cherry lozenges between the tongue
and roof of the chapelmaster, the pitched poor quality singing

of a kindergartner, dust vanished in the new constructions,
a bird of paradox held up to the light version of the program,

the shortened Magic Flute with puppets for inattentive kids;
being a dick to someone by deliberately lying about something

that there's no reason to lie about except that you're bored and sun
streams in and you fancy yourself a verbose engine of consciousness

from those summers of exponential sickness, or the woman inside the rip-off
impressionist painting you bought last year at the Cleveland Meridian,

because the image of her hung over your head like a rain
cloud in a cartoon since that Monday as if a memory, but really,

a beautiful nude is in the mirror every morning if you wish,
a beautiful day hangs beneath the thirteen-odd billion years

of space in every direction, you're at the fulcral joint of chaos,
the wig on the statue, the plummet lines of dead cells anointing

its forehead, both flesh and idea, jerry-built chambers of sound, voice boxes,
pretty, muscular signers of contracts with the biggies, true horror

lovers pining for the next crime to be serialized and twirled into
a milkshake-like roulette noir jangling its silver bullet

which tastes of spoiled lager, look, I'm a visiting professor
of nothing at the University of Nowhere, and as I type this in

the branches of the algorithm fire like short-order cooks
to the server looking for the perfect March apple blossom amber

eating away at her pigtails, trust there will always be a slowdown, a rest
period, to initialize the consolidation of wealth, allow the openings

of newer, eliter pre-K environments for organically outfitted children
running out of the gates like perfect storms, till the land grabs

them, and the wicked combine of rock and gravity pops against their soles—
the miner's lowest veins, the valley's navel, stretching the skin

of buildable land across quicksand, sinkholes, imaginary silos—
to go mad means different things in the bell chain's diminishing range,

ion etchings on the eardrums, erosion at all distal points, Sunday
turns itself into fantasy almost by instinct, world after world,

the infinity of possibilities is vastly outnumbered by the infinity
of impossibilities, of what dissolves into zero at the edges

of our visions, storytellers cash in stacked decks: an Andalusian cruise,
aleatory death maps, Mandelbrot's candelabras, mortuarial rehearsals

following exhumations in the name of scientific advances, delusions
of paradise, merry, humming, vestigially coded into the unreal,

like nymphs, parentless daughters—something, a dream, a buzzing,
a scrap of pink powdery vellum on the breakfast table by the Casio

digital watch and coffee mug attached to the parental appendage
that the randomizer caught and chewed into magic—something,

a dream, a buzzing, a mountain of clothing—dress shirts and other shit—
a limitless line of loafers—jogging shoes and other shit—a prayer

within the empty closet that when the door reopens another world
will have set in: the door reopens to a veranda over mountains,

green as parrot feathers; the door reopens to a marble apartment
where an intuitive Catalan woman offers me a glass of instant

lemonade; the door reopens and reopens like a dead man's suitcase,
always changing its contents, its knowledge of me diminishing

with every turn, they forget you, renaming a child
when the closet world, the world of turning portals, succumbs

to economic realities, shifting flood zones, lamenting gaps
in his translated works, delays in object permanence, wondering

if that child on the floor is really yours, still resisting the briefly
inescapable fact of your having had been here at this very moment.

· · ·

Lyme Chronicles

J. calls at nine, waking the infant,
From a bar outside Austin.

He says, "I'm in heaven."
My Bloody Valentine plays in the distance.

"It's been eight years," I say.
Like it hasn't been a day.

. . .

He calls again, collect, in a wiry voice.
"I've met this girl in Park City.

She sells pottery with witty shit
Written on it." The noise

Of semis flies through the phone.
I can't hear the rest so keep saying, "I know."

. . .

J. calls two years later,
In the a.m. I've left my new iPhone

By the bed. The second infant
Sleeps through it, but the toddler

Wakes, and she goes to check on him.
For a long time, he doesn't say anything.

. . .

"Where are you calling from?"
"Don't know man, where you?"

"I'm home. Dude,
What's going on?"

"Nothing." J. hangs up.
I read my phone till she comes back.

. . .

I'm googling concussions in three-year-olds
When another number crosses the stream.

I feel like I haven't talked to a soul in weeks.
A Nevada area code.

If it's J., I can't handle it.
I let it go to voicemail.

. . .

Each time I talk to someone I know
I learn how little they know me.

I'm surprised fish still exist.
I've no proof I have a soul.

I feel like soul is the wrong word.
I feel I've made a turn into the wrong world.

. . .

"A week after the boy was born
I ran into Jamie outside the pool hall,"

I tell J. He calls
At a good time, mid-morning.

Everyone's at school.
"He looked like hell."

. . .

J. sounds good, I think.
I barely let him talk.

I go on and on about kids,
Like I'm the first and only

Father in the fucking world.
I think he's suicidal.

. . .

J.'s thinking of suicide,
but he won't let on.

I might be wrong.
It's all in my mind.

The lyrics of turn-of-the-century alt-rock songs
Are all I can think in these days.

. . .

I haven't told you about J.
I haven't told anyone.

Maybe he's an illusion.
I don't think I should.

I doubt I've ever cared.
Anyway, I'm incapable of love.

. . .

Do you have that thing?
You worry if you say what's on your mind

People might come for you?
White guys in white coats, waiting

With chains, just outside the room.
Everyone expects the Spanish Inquisition.

. . .

I lie in the doctor's office, a real doctor
And everything: tissue paper over

A baby-blue plastic vinyl cushion.
I feel like I just drank desiccant.

I hear my heart/phone vibrate
In my pants slung on the wall.

. . .

"I saw a tree growing trout from its boughs,"
J. says, "birthing them all in the space

Of an hour. Turning in place
Like small buds, the tiny heads of trout

Coming like corkscrews, till the fully formed fish swayed
Like tackle from the bending rods of the trout tree."

. . .

I think the doctor thinks I'm crazy.
I offer it up as a possibility

Because I'm nervous, and he agrees
Without saying it. He plays vague.

"Pain," he says, "is the mind mostly . . ."
"Like J.," I reply.

. . .

"If fish are the shapes of leaves,
Maybe they were parts of a larger life-form

That broke off and started to swim?"
"The heart is leaf shaped, maybe we

Are just rampant overgrowth?"
"How does life in air and water differ in breath?"

. . .

I wish I was stoned.
The last time I smoked

I couldn't breathe for weeks.
Then we moved inland for a semester,

Thinking things would be easier.
The body is a wind instrument.

. . .

Slowly, I feel I'm manufacturing
An insanity plea for some unforeseen thing

I'm going to do.
My tongue is leaf shaped.

Maybe it is a fish.
Maybe you are a trout tree.

. . .

J. doesn't call for too long.
I'm afraid to tell her

My tongue burns. I'm acting off-kilter,
And the kids don't understand.

I lie in bed with my iPhone,
Looking at colorful pictures of trout.

. . .

I google J. because I won't do Facebook,
But his name's too common.

I google Common and learn
We share the same birthday,

But he's a year older
And much taller and better looking.

. . .

I tend to let go of friends.
Like shedding skin.

When I was a kid I was sure
If I disappeared

No one would notice.
I doubt they'll grow up before I die.

. . .

"Our bodies are colonies, J.,"
I say aloud to you.

"Who is J.?" you ask.
He's a colony off the Americas . . .

"Being a child is terrifying,"
I say finally.

. . .

J. will call.
As sure as the future is here.

We are in the future,
So our actions doesn't matter

Anymore, they just occur
Before us like a movie trailer.

. . .

Without telling their mother
I tell the kids J.

Is my invisible friend.
They think it's real funny.

I wish I was in love with him.
Reality has its imitations.

. . .

J. calls out of nowhere
Like he always does.

I literally can't move because
Lyme has crossed the blood-

Brain barrier. I don't want to know
What other people's lives are like.

. . .

"I used to fish for trout
In a lake in Vermont.

The whole thing felt staged
Like 'this is what families do.'

I was only six,
But I knew it was bullshit."

. . .

"Bringing kids into this world . . ."
"I know. It's delusional,

This hope that it will all
Turn out ok." "Your body unwinds

Like a bad joke." "Alien strands
Of RNA drilling into me.

. . .

Gradually I've turned into this host
Accumulating coinfections

Like dominoes, once it hits
The nervous system/string section,

You can't tell if it's live or Memorex,
Phantom or pathogen, like a mixtape

. . .

Infinitely looping, pooling biofilms,
Everything I see steeped in halos

Of hydroxychloroquine retinal stains,
Spirochetes gnawing on my optic lines,

Straining under sunlight, gaslight, maybe it's just
Garden variety anxiety

. . .

So I should shut the fuck up.
Neuropathy builds you a silent dimension.

Silos the nowhere of being ill.
I doubt J. believes any of this is real.

I don't think anyone will get the joke
That is me.

. . .

J. says the problem is me.
The truth, I say, is like salt

Dissolving in your mouth
As you eat a block of maple sugar

Shaped like a maple leaf
Instead of a trout."

...

Virtual Terminal

Light information flowers
For the terror in the mirror.

Beautiful creatures, sentences circle
You like carrion birds.

Round your black helix hair
Shining like money

Like the moon's a coin
With an emperor's face

Scratched down to the base.
Time is memory.

Antwerp

The Governor's eyelids were coming apart
In small pieces; we hardly noticed it.

He remarked on his daughter's rapid change
Of hair color after she began seeing

The quiet film director from Antwerp.
She had been blonde as ash just weeks ago.

Meeting with his advisors and adversaries, sigh,
I noticed a well of saline in the garden

Where various amphibians grew.
I held my penlight and iodine dropper

Above the well—I had been seeing flashes
Of white and dark spots at my periphery

For weeks and feared a detached retina,
But I'd no time to go to the guy—

At a drop of iodine, the eggs began
To shiver, and I felt a very cold season

Enter my life, followed by a hand grasping
My side, under my ribs, very close to the liver.

I called Sarah on her cell; it didn't help.
A second hand, no less real, tapped me

On the bone at the edge of my neck.
A small woman smiled uncomfortably,

Her teeth elaborately wired,
"Sir . . . J____," she said, "we're waiting."

. . .

Near the Governor's desk there's a sketch;
Some claim it's an early van Gogh,

But never the Governor.
It's of ordered rows of tulips, each

Marked with a letter: G for *yellow,*
C for *blue,* R for *rood.* There's a woman

(V for *woman*) wearing a woven hood.
"You see her?" he said.

"She doesn't feel much, she has no words,
She just deposits him in the flower beds,

Do you see?" I didn't. But I listened
Carefully, climbed on the first

Train to Antwerp, and fired a Kimber
1911 twice into the director's chest.

At first it fixed everything, like a strong
Medicine washing over the symptoms.

. . .

I returned to the daughter.
She was atrophied; cellophane covered

Her hands. I could feel her heart move
At the divisions. I said, "Do you feel

Like something else is in you, holding you?"
"Not like love?" she asked. "No, not at all."

We kissed. Our lips and tongues
So dry, we barely felt it. "Your father,

He used to like me so much.
Now everyone is distant, everyone

Looks at me like I'm missing something."
I wanted her to reach in

And pull the hand out of me. I looked
At her organs, a menagerie of small

Birds and mammals locked in various stages
Of prenatal growth. "I don't like to feed them,"

She said. "They're building a wall
Around Antwerp. They loved the director.

They're afraid of losing anything else . . .
No one wants to make sense of it . . .

We're the keepers of our soils." She cinched
The yellow rope inside her hoodie.

. . .

I traveled by ferry to Copenhagen, on a seasonless
Day, to a square at the center of the city

Where a nineteenth-century building
Bore my name in plaster at the cornice.

I had dyed my hair the opposite color
Of what it had been before Antwerp,

But a man recognized me because of my eyes.
He pressed his hand into my ribs.

I bit my lip. "Tender," he said.
He took me to his flat and served

Me schnapps. I lay in his bed and kissed
His eyelid—the room was white

As blue milk, French windows,
Long skating curtains—and felt the eye dart

Uncomfortably underneath, looking
At a memory of a film from the 50s

Which I haven't seen.
I told him about the tulips. The moon

Was common. He mentioned Hammershøi
And the cold resistance to dreams.

"Why is this happening?" I asked. "It's the future,"
He said. "Everything happens in the future."

Persephone

daughter time cuts the rhyme.

a mouthful asphodel
harsh marble polish
slickers on and orange eyelets
trick the pixels into flies.

see-through thoughts catch
stipple bruising on the moth's edge
ruby calyx tubing
diamond skinned drill fish
rivers sip on shallow glasses
surfacing to ankle height.

lowering the chin to the heart
the forehead enters summer.

incursions down the hillsides
glaucous flowers, phosphorous
opening your hair
to the aerosol air
fairy clocks
and the rest is luck.

sepal of the lithosphere
beaded by the aether
where the ghosts of men appear
skin as thin paper
is the record in the letter,
blood, or knots of wood
burnt on her clothes.

girls slip through
the flow of morning traffic.

a soldier feeds pomegranate seeds
and water to kiss.

horizon razor and wire
the camera's eye captures
fissures in the code
sunlight through a punctured sleeve

no snow
on her sparrow-brown
shoulders

braided radioisotopes
breath-like whips
of almost frozen lake weeds
whistling blue corneal film

the earth split like eyelids
purple pools of pupil oil
unspeaking, leafless foil

Albedo

A green TV lake taken with methamphetamine
Birds' feet in spring shadowpaths of ice
Cities' ecstatic stalagmitic mimicry
Dreaming meaning into every search and capture
Endlessly excerpted as the continuum is impossible to sustain
Fingers clicking like cricket legs on the keyboard
Grain lands in random arrangements like marriages
House of a thousand worlds
Inflorescences of midsummer purple on the green milk thistle
Jackhammers like cicadas in the distance
Kids drip Mountain Dew on an ant hill to see what comes
Laughter from rum till sundown, tide up
Moon pool, a shaft through a drilling rig
Nothing ceases
1
Powerlessness is equivalent to the barbarities
Quilting the village of unending consciousness
Reading water like it's text
Slowly falling cotton lands on her orange puffer
Tim leaves his amorous lilt on Lily's machine
Utopias in glass bottle Cokes with real sugar from Mexico
Van Gogh's yellow halos in the soft slides between saccades
Waves of wheat fields weave through the optic axis
Xanthopsia being the convenient diagnosis
Yellow foxglove bells ring around his eyes
o

<g><r><a><y><w><i><t><h><m><o><o><n><l><i><g><h><t>
<a><n><d><s><h><e><l><o><o><k><s><m><e><o><v><e><r>
<c><h><i><l><d><o><n><t><h><e><s><u><r><f><a><c><e>
<o><f><m><y><e><y><e><s><a><s><i><f><t><o><s><a><y>
<a><r><e><w><e><s><t><i><l><l><o><n><e><a><r><t><h>
<t><h><e><s><o><u><n><d><s><o><f><l><e><a><v><e><s>
<f><e><r><r><i><s><w><h><e><e><l><f><l><a><r><e><s>
<s><o><m><e><w><h><e><r><e><b><e><h><i><n><d><m><e>
<i><l><i><g><h><t><a><s><m><a><l><l><f><l><a><m><e>
<o><n><h><e><r><b><a><n><g><s><a><n><d><t><a><m><p>
<i><t><w><i><t><h><m><y><p><a><l><m><s><h><e><i><s>
<n><o><t><o><n><e><b><i><t><s><t><a><r><t><l><e><d>
<j><u><s><t><l><o><s><t><i><n><t><h><o><u><g><h><t>
<l><o><s><t><w><i><t><h><i><n><h><e><r><s><e><l><f>
<t><e><s><t><i><n><g><t><h><e><r><e><a><l><i><t><y>
<s><o><m><e><w><h><e><r><e><i><n><a><h><o><t><e><l>
<t><e><r><r><a><c><e><s><t><h><a><t><g><l><i><n><t>
<w><h><e><n><t><h><e><c><l><o><u><d><s><p><a><r><t>
<o><n><a><b><l><u><e><n><i><g><h><t><s><t><a><n><d>
<a><l><u><m><i><n><u><m><w><r><a><p><p><i><n><g><s>
<w><i><t><h><i><l><l><u><s><t><r><a><t><i><o><n><s>
<o><f><s><t><r><a><w><b><e><r><r><i><e><s><a><n><d>
<r><e><d><g><i><n><g><e><r><b><r><e><a><d><m><e><n>
<t><h><e><l><e><t><e><t><t><e><r><s><t><r><i><c><k><l><e>
<t><h><r><o><u><g><h><t><h><e><c><e><i><l><i><n><g>
<t><h><e><i><r><s><h><a><d><o><w><s><l><e><a><v><e>
<t><h><e><i><r><s><h><a><l><l><o><w><s><o><n><m><e>
<s><h><e><t><e><l><l><s><m><e><t><h><e><k><i><d><s>
<a><r><e><i><n><t><h><e><o><t><h><e><r><r><o><o><m>
<d><r><e><s><s><e><d><i><n><l><a><n><g><u><a><g><e>
<o><n><e><a><t><o><m><t><h><i><c><k><s><t><r><i><p>
<o><f><g><r><a><p><h><e><n><e><l><a><t><t><i><c><e>
<i><f><w><e><c><o><u><l><d><d><i><s><s><o><l><v><e>

<a><m><o><n><g><t><h><e><a><l><p><h><a><b><e><t><s>
<t><h><e><y><o><u><n><g><e><r><o><n><e><s><e><e><s>
<a><b><i><r><d><s><r><e><s><e><m><b><l><a><n><c><e>
<t><o><a><l><e><t><t><e><r><i><n><m><o><t><i><o><n>
<i><n><t><h><e><i><r><o><w><n><t><o><n><g><u><e><s>
<t><h><e><t><r><e><e><s><g><r><o><w><c><o><d><e><s>
<f><r><o><m><t><h><e><i><r><b><r><a><n><c><h><e><s>
<i><m><a><g><i><n><e><s><o><m><e><o><n><e><y><o><u>
<l><e><a><v><e><a><l><o><n><e><t><o><o><l><o><n><g>
<l><e><a><v><e><a><l><o><n><e><a><s><e><c><o><n><d>
<l><e><a><v><e><a><l><e><t><t><e><r><i><n><t><h><e>
<m><i><d><d><l><e><o><f><t><h><e><b><a><n><k><o><f>
<t><h><e><r><i><v><e><r><l><i><k><e><l><i><n><e><s>
<s><e><e><t><h><e><s><o><n><i><c><t><h><r><e><a><d>
<a><s><s><h><e><s><e><e><s><t><h><e><w><o><o><d><s>
<d><e><n><a><t><u><r><a><l><i><z><e><d><p><a><l><e>
<i><j><u><s><t><t><h><o><u><g><h><t><a><b><o><u><t>
<y><o><u><a><n><d><y><o><u><t><e><x><t><e><d><m><e>
<i><b><e><l><i><e><v><e><d><t><h><e><g><a><p><i><n>
<m><y><e><a><r><s><w><a><s><w><h><e><r><e><a><l><l>
<t><h><e><w><i><n><d><i><n><t><h><e><w><o><r><l><d>
<w><a><s><k><i><d><s><s><t><a><y><a><s><l><e><e><p>
<a><l><l><s><p><e><c><i><e><s><s><t><i><l><l><o><n>
<m><y><d><a><u><g><h><t><e><r><t><e><l><l><s><m><e>
<s><h><e><w><a><s><a><n><a><l><i><e><n><j><u><s><t>
<f><l><o><a><t><i><n><g><s><o><m><e><w><h><e><r><e>
<c><l><o><s><e><t><o><m><y><s><h><o><u><l><d><e><r>
<a><n><d><s><w><i><m><m><i><n><g><i><g><u><e><s><s>
<i><n><o><t><h><e><r><s><u><b><s><t><r><a><t><e><s>
<w><a><k><i><n><g><t><h><r><o><u><g><h><a><s><e><a>
<c><o><v><e><r><i><n><g><m><y><e><y><e><s><f><o><r>
<m><e><w><i><t><h><o><u><t><a><n><y><h><a><n><d><s>

Moon Pool

tungsten floodlight forklift sky rift hollow
glades
through cloud breaks follow
spill to
the moon pool
down the drill ship's spinal column up
the brain's statistical seascape's sable currents culling silver stemmed lilies of life data
dayglo igloos
light up southern satellite states all night long sonic booms rip sound waves apart
like the hearts
broken on track 3
to be repaired on track 5
following the instrumental interlude
in dusk all cats are blue
flute suites rise
cellos mix segmented fingertips
gut core strings and skin cells' long strand dna beaches crept on all fours
listening from my velvet sofa
quick and lethal
mercury in the water table
delivered by sublingual placebo
trickling placid gusts of cold nickel lithium change down the coin slot of the soda
machine
cymbals clamber up nerve scales
wading
wide seas of unseeable chemicals
a satellite drops into the ocean
crosses the sky
gray skeins
wake streams
from the engine's alembic
slices past a silver surfer piping through a wave off Mozambique
her watertight wetsuit screen printed with satinette
and nikko blue hydrangeas

made translucent by sun and brine
light chloride hair
empire waist
paraben laced skin over all things
radium palladium iridium forever molecules fluorosurfactants
trace
a face in your hands across the seafloor's mines
there isn't an infinity of riches beneath/within us
so small it feels like there is
not knowing how/where i'll lose you
how/where i'll stop losing you/us
the day goes whiter than before
ghostwriter
keeps erasing itself
water to her ears
inside her ears
blood music swells thin tinny plush copper wash
no objective way to measure pain/joy
escape
slide toward the silent mouth of the curve
sunless zones where falling things keep slower falling
fathom where there is
if there is
a terminus
motionless mythless witness
distance
at the extremity of a line in space
and do you remember any
time dripping drifting ripple apple lipid paper vapor bodies scattered in full blown
fever plumb the chutes through which other realms unspool
any alternate dimension would be an uninhabitable shell of pneumatic breath travel
drill drill duct tube trough spirit
air seeps in speaks in your bones
runaway

heat melt flood lust despair law chance texts playing dice with algorithms
algae blooms
algebra means to mend the broken thing the missing thing substitute like for like
restore the torn unseen mutable mercurial variable x or y or whatever i.e.
you
nowhere to disappear to
a ten gallon drum
the plane's wings tilt starboard
the sky is a drowning
blue

Antwerp

Whenever I went on too long about Antwerp
The doctor would quietly descend the two steps

To the kitchen and pour a cold French white
Into a tumbler, so as not to incriminate himself.

There was a growing sense of foreign matter
In my body, a sense that the divisions between

Old friends and this new emptiness . . .
That the daughter had lied to me about Antwerp.

In the disquiet after the director's burial
No one built a wall,

Just a subtle tuning up of the collective
Feeling of justice when preying

On the visibly foreign.
It would be noticeably felt for a few years

Until fading into a newer baseline noise
Peculiar to the city

Like the taste of its tap water in the bread.
"It wasn't blindness exactly," the doctor said.

"The Governor's eyes. Just the inability
To translate light, to differentiate hue."

He sipped his wine like one whose job
Was finished.

The next morning, we began
Calling each other by different names.

. . .

The seasons were blending as the angle of the sun
Seemed a gesture. The ferry recrossed

The waters below Denmark. The man who checked
My passport seemed troubled by my eyes.

On a bench beside a marine-blue travel bag
A woman glared anxiously at them

And whispered, "J____?"
Her dental work was gone.

Her teeth resembled weathered churchyard pales.
Her mouth closed, and her eyes moved

Off mine. I stood by the railing facing south,
The isle of Fehmarn approaching fast.

. . .

I arrived at the director's apartment
The next day. It had been three months

Since he was shot by an unknown assailant,
A man with only a vague description:

White, medium height, medium weight, wiry
Like the director. A few potted flowers,

Azaleas and irises, remained on the street,
Where an impassable shrine had clogged foot traffic.

The intercom panel at the doorway still
Bore the director's name, as did a rough makeshift

Plaque below it. "The Imaginary Walls
Of Antwerp," I said to myself. A tall woman

In a long beige coat passed me, her heels clicking
Away, paused briefly as she looked back

To observe me enter the building.
The stairwell had been repainted

Since my last visit.
It was a nicer color than before, calmer.

I felt I'd entered a grand nursery,
Ascending a hanging spiral mobile of stairs.

. . .

The apartment was nearly unchanged.
Nothing boxed, little altered.

It was cleaner. Music
Played on a phonograph. An early piano

Recording of something nineteenth century.
A vase filled with dried flowers still sat on

The dining table, veiny purple.
The place smelled different, fresher and salty

Like taffy like old skim milk like Indian tea
Like powdered clothing and clear alcohol.

A woman was sitting at the table
Just to the left of the vase,

Looking into me as if I was part
Transparent and part shadow,

Like I was a ghost.
"What's happened to your eyes?" she finally said.

The doctor had said he could fix everything
Except the eyes.

She sat there, the director's mother, convinced
She'd woken up within a dream she couldn't

Leave, the wrinkled skin of burnt milk rippling
On half the surface of her tea. She continued

Looking blankly over my features till
She was certain what stood before her

Was exactly what her son would look like
Upon returning from the sere regions.

One of his films was about
Just such a thing. A man, without dialogue,

Returns to his family three months after being
Shot fatally by a terrorist. After

The initial shock and panic, his presence
Is accepted, tacitly, and family life

Quietly reassumes.
"You look the same. Like your movie."

I nodded. She rose, no longer looking,
And disappeared into the kitchen, returning

With a cup and saucer, which she placed
Before me without a word. I sat and sipped

The burnt milky flavor of honey and twigs.
I felt more like myself than I had in years.

...

Super Fragile Catalyst

our child was the size of a hummingbird
neatly glued to the stomach lining

blur of liquid metal sunshine
purring through apse and radial cells

a gently rising submarine
in the unsettling before sleep

a hologram of your next self
will break into a new body

building a raceme hierarchy
from which the hummingbird sips

a race disappears around the corner
I hear their voices another two blocks

colors at sunset go from the schoolyard
skin dusted shades of cobalt

river sounds flow out of eyeshot
a heart-based curvature of time (language)

a contraction of time (systole) in the heart
hearing the kids fly from imaginary beings

the filling of time or blood (diastole)
in a name you dream walks by you

new love flutters at seventy wingbeats
a new movie flickers at twenty-four flames

a thousand fine gradations of happiness
performing a lice check on my daughter

testing all twenty-six teeth
in the Latin alphabet

the tongue like a Ouija planchette
points to the letter it licks

a silverleaf-faced angel pricks
her finger with a sterile need

missing rivers of bodies flow
through channels of the blood

are you so different having seen the second
beating of a wing across the shoulder

a woman once came to our apartment
all the bones in China wouldn't bend

a vivid pink against the cheek that way
a swan rustles in the neoprene

our minds better at absorbing
fictions than new realities

shivering snare drum
phantom living lung

flawless sun-like figurines
sea-level dreaming azimuths

synthetic hyacinth junk derivatives
finite winter maize red party

black famine roulette station pilgrims
live hierarchical prunings in the brain

diving bells locked in palatine eardrums
a serpentine train set carries us off

decidual trans-cysteine life machines
cosmetic metalinguistic surgery prongs

sword-forged consanguine molecular
carbon substitutions on a benzene ring

polyphonic fucking data strata erotics
sugar tongs orange gin red sangria

funny how gallium melts in the palm
how a human head melts in the mind

anything can be anything else after burning
the key to metamorphosis is turning

drawn without learning the lettering
the alternate editing the director's cut

written in heaven among the bodies
of the 24 episodes to come

and bead upon be cloned among
other things a turnip plant an explosive device

the impulse to cloak the exposed girl
super fragile catalysts

to rout to expel the Red Cross
wear whiteface be cow eyed to desert to echo

a corpse looks nothing like a robot
the sight of corpses is commoner

in less industrialized nations
the presence of the illusion

of distance deepens the assimilation
of the angel's silver leafed plane

the wind's a substitution for the sonic gulf
where water ran above us

but then again upon waking I lose
the conviction

where the wind farm is now
not far from the radiowaste tanks

a man once returned to the edge
of a battlefield made silver

by meadows filled with bodies
whose noses or ears were severed

as tokens by victors and carried
in sacks to later match to the kill

the man filled with hunger
held a yuzu rind against his teeth

the unimaginable being
the reality I choose

not to process the eyes'
aversion to the thing I

cordon off whole sections of
the body rendered herded

speechless unheard of zoned
imagining reality as it cones

in the quarter-second brain delay
by the phenotype's deficiency

where does the mapping end
all the thoughtless forms formed from foam

glaring indifferently like 1000 toys
glaring happily like 100000 toys

unimagined casualties
rolling through watery air

freshly minted tongues for kissing
behind the schoolyard

fuck and dream of continuities
between impassable mirrors

I worry when you lift your eyes to this you
won't find a satisfying mirror

I was reading about kindness last night
the currency in the early minds of kids

I thought the animals outside
were dressed in human conditions

I thought of writing a treatment
for an animated sitcom

in which everything is normal as hell
but everyone's all dressed up as animals

ACKNOWLEDGMENTS

My deepest gratitude to the editors of the following journals for publishing versions of poems from this book:

Conjunctions: "The Atlas of Virtual" and "Super Fragile Catalyst"
New Yorker: "To a Kid Launched One Year after the iPhone"
Paris Review: the second poem titled "Antwerp"

I am eternally grateful to Chicu Reddy, Katie Peterson, Rosa Alcalá, and Doug Kearney for their amazing belief in and support of this work—and to all the editors and the board of the University of Chicago Press for making this happen.

Effusive thanks to Chicu, Mark Levine, Arda Collins, and Ema Yamashiro for their invaluable feedback at various key points/nodes/stations throughout the journey of this thing.

Thanks to Chris Chen, Cathy Hong, Jieho Lee, Sandra Miller, and so many friends, writers, and creators who have moved me in countless directions over these years.

Thanks to my colleagues and students at Parsons, the New School, and Columbia for furthering my explorations of the computational imagination.

Thank you to the doctors and medical professionals who believed me, listened, and brought their imaginations, skills, and compassion to my "case" over the past decade.

Infinite love to my family for constantly inspiring this work and me. And especially, and most of all, to Ema, for carrying me through.

NOTES

The titles for "Perceptron," "Deep Mind," and "Deep Dream" are drawn from the history of AI neural networks. The perceptron was originally proposed by Frank Rosenblatt in 1962. DeepMind, an AI research lab, was first established in 2010, before Google acquired it. DeepDream, a computer vision program, was first released by Google in 2015.